❦ History *of* Britain ❦

The Stuarts

1603 to 1714

Andrew Langley

HAMLYN

HISTORY OF BRITAIN – STUARTS
was produced for Hamlyn Children's Books
by Lionheart Books, London.

Editor: Lionel Bender
Designer: Ben White
Picture Researcher: Jennie Karrach
Media Conversion and Typesetting:
    Peter MacDonald and Una Macnamara

Educational Consultant: Jane Shuter

Production Controller: Linda Spillane
Managing Editor: David Riley

First Published in Great Britain in 1993
by Hamlyn Children's Books,
an imprint of Reed Children's Books Limited,
Michelin House, 81 Fulham Road, London SW3 6RB,
and Auckland, Melbourne, Singapore and Toronto.

Copyright © 1993 Reed International Books Limited.

ISBN 0 600 58026 1 (PB)   ISBN 0 600 58027 X (HB)

British Library Cataloguing-in-Publication Data. A catalogue
record for this book is available from the British Library.

Acknowledgements
Photo credits: From His Grace, Duke of Atholl's Collection, Blair
Castle, Perthshire: page 6. By courtesy of the National Portrait
Gallery, London: pages: 12, 20 (top), 25, 30. Fotomas Index:
pages 13, 14 (left), 18, 19, 24. The Royal Collection © 1993 Her
Majesty the Queen: page 31. The Mansell Collection: pages 8, 9,
14 (right), 15, 20 (bottom), 21, 28, 34, 38, 40, 42. Courtesy of
the Trustees of The British Museum: page 11. e.t archive: page
16. Heinemann Educational/Ashmolean Museum, Oxford: page
22. Courtesy of the Record Office, House of Lords: page 23.
Michael Holford: pages 27, 41. By Permission of the Birmingham
Museum and Art Gallery: page 32. Reproduced with the
permission of the Trustees of National Library of Scotland: page
33. The Bridgeman Art Library: page 37 top (Courtesy of Bristol
Museum & Art Gallery) and bottom, page 39, pages 40-41
(Courtesy of National Army Museum, London), Ann Ronan
Picture Library/Image Select: page 43 (top).
Cover: Bridgeman Art Library, Michael Holford, Fotomas Index;
artwork by Stephen Conlin.
Artwork: Stefan Chabluk: all maps. Mark Bergin: pages 12-13,
24-25, 38-39. James Field: pages 14-15, 18-19, 20-21, 42-43,
46. Nick Hewetson: pages 8-9, 30-31, 40-41. John James: pages
1, 2, 5, 6-7, 10-11, 16-17, 22-23, 26-27, 28-29, 32-33, 34-35,
36-37. Malcolm Smythe: page 45. Haywood Art: page 44.

CONTENTS

The Stuart Period
During the Stuart period there were many changes which shaped the way we live today. The photographs in this book are mostly of buildings and objects from that time.

The illustrations in this book are based on historical evidence. They have been painted by artists who have used drawings and descriptions from Stuart times to help them to decide how things would have looked then.

ROMAN BRITAIN 55BC to AD406	SAXONS AND VIKINGS 406 to 1066	THE MIDDLE AGES 1066 to 1485	THE TUDORS 1485 to 1603	THE STUARTS 1603 to 1714	THE GEORGIANS 1714 to 1837	VICTORIAN BRITAIN 1837 to 1901	MODERN BRITAIN 1901 to the 1990s

ABOUT THIS BOOK

This book considers the Stuarts chronologically, meaning that events are described in the order in which they happened, from 1603 to 1714. Most of the double-page articles deal with a particular part of Stuart history. Those that deal with aspects of everyday life, such as trade, houses and clothing, are more general and cover the whole period. This is because these things did not change each time a new king or queen came to the throne. Unfamiliar words are explained in the glossary on page 46.

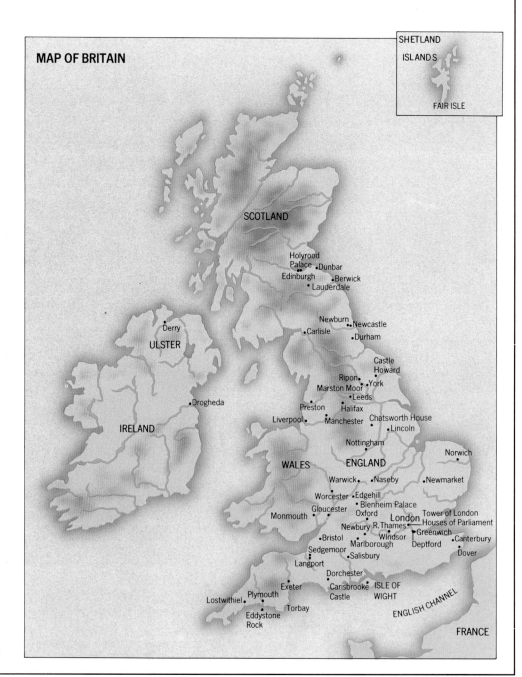

MAP OF BRITAIN

SHETLAND ISLANDS

FAIR ISLE

SCOTLAND

Holyrood Palace • • Dunbar
Edinburgh • • Berwick
• Lauderdale

Newburn • • Newcastle
• Carlisle • Durham

Derry •

ULSTER

Castle Howard •
Ripon • • York
Marston Moor • • Leeds
Preston • Halifax •
Liverpool • • Manchester • Chatsworth House
• Lincoln

Drogheda •

IRELAND

Nottingham •

Norwich •

WALES   ENGLAND

Warwick • • Naseby   • Newmarket
Worcester • • Edgehill
• Blenheim Palace
Gloucester • Oxford   Tower of London
Monmouth •   London • Houses of Parliament
Newbury • R. Thames • • Greenwich
• Bristol   • Windsor   • Deptford   • Canterbury
Sedgemoor • Marlborough   • Dover
Langport •   • Salisbury
Dorchester •
Exeter •   Carisbrooke
Lostwithiel •   Plymouth •   • Castle   ISLE OF WIGHT
Eddystone   Torbay •   ENGLISH CHANNEL
Rock
FRANCE

About the map

This shows the location of places mentioned in the text. Some are major cities, others towns or the sites of battles or famous buildings.

INTRODUCTION

The Stuart kings and queens reigned from 1603 to 1714. This was a time of great upheavals. One king was beheaded (Charles I in 1649), and another was forced to give up the throne (James II in 1688). All the Stuarts were short of money, and made themselves unpopular by raising taxes. England was a firmly Protestant country, and Roman Catholics and Puritans suffered persecution. The biggest struggle of all was between Crown and Parliament. This boiled up into a civil war in 1642. Parliament won, and for 11 years Britain was without a monarch.

But Britain also grew much stronger during the 17th century. It became the most important trading nation in Europe. England and Scotland were united under the same king. British colonies were founded in North America. Towards the end of the Stuart period, Britain's army defeated France in two wars, and the navy took control of the seas. This was also an age of great scientists, including Isaac Newton and William Harvey.

The reign of the Stuarts began with high hopes. On 26 March 1603, a horseman arrived at Holyrood Palace in Edinburgh. He told the Scottish king, James VI, that Queen Elizabeth was dead. James was now King of England as well. His mother had been Mary, Queen of Scots, Elizabeth's cousin. Because Elizabeth had had no children, James was her nearest relative. Many English people were delighted to have a king at last, after two queens. They were glad, too, that James had no rivals for the throne. He seemed to be a strong and clever king.

JAMES I 1603 – 1625

"Kings are not only God's lieutenants on Earth, and sit upon God's throne, but even by God himself they are called gods." – said by James I to Parliament in 1610. King James was 37 years old when he set out for London. Many people came to greet him on the road.

James was not very kingly to look at. He had large, rolling eyes and spindly legs. He dressed sloppily, and rarely washed. His strong Scots accent was hard for many to understand. Although well-educated and clever, he was arrogant and lazy. He thought that kings were appointed by God, and could do as they wished. The new king also lost people's respect by giving money and power to favourites at court. He made George Villiers Duke of Buckingham in 1623. Villiers became his closest advisor.

▷ **James leaves Holyrood Castle** on his way to London. He had been king of Scotland since 1567, when he was a baby. His childhood was lonely and unhappy. As an adult, he ruled Scotland cleverly. He turned his enemies against each other and gained control of part of the Highlands and Western Isles. But, after 1603, he only came back to Scotland once for a brief visit in 1617.

△ **A King James VI** of Scotland coin.

▷ **James with his mother Mary**, Queen of Scots. James never saw her after 1567, so this portrait is imaginary. Mary was beheaded by the English for treason on 8 February 1587.

The new king thought that England was a rich country. But Elizabeth had left large debts, and James was extravagant. His coronation cost £20,000, and he spent lavishly on hunting and banquets. By 1610, he was so short of money that he forced City banks to give him loans and sold titles for £1,000 a time.

He also increased his income by raising the customs duties on imported goods. The Members of Parliament (MPs) argued that the king could not raise taxes without their permission. And they became angry when James lectured them about his Divine Right to rule his subjects as he wanted.

In 1611, the king sent Parliament away and tried to govern by himself. But still he struggled to find enough money. His taxes and forced loans were unpopular. Meanwhile, the gap widened between the Crown and Parliament.

James tried to avoid expensive wars by:
● ending the long conflict with Spain in 1604
● attempting to make peace between Spain and Holland in 1609
● bringing Catholic and Protestant countries together by marriage. He planned to marry his eldest son Henry to a Catholic Spanish princess. His daughter Elizabeth married a German Protestant prince. But Henry died. And the German prince became King of Bohemia, but was soon driven out by the Catholic emperor of Austria in 1618.

THE GUNPOWDER PLOT 1605

Laws against Catholics in England had been harsh during Elizabeth I's reign. They had been fined for not going to church, and were not allowed to hold their own services. When James became king, he made vague promises about giving the Catholics freedom to worship as they wanted.

But the king never kept his promise. He knew that most people would protest at a move to help the Catholics. Instead, his chief minister, Robert Cecil, made the penalties more severe. He increased the fines and banished all Catholic priests.

In 1604, a group of Catholics plotted their revenge. They were led by Robert Catesby. Their plan had two parts. First, they would blow up the House of Lords on 5 November 1605. This was the opening day of Parliament, when MPs, the Lords, and the king himself, would be there. Secondly, they would start a Catholic rising in the Midlands and drive James from the throne.

▷ **The plotters** hired a building next to Parliament and tried to dig a tunnel beneath the House of Lords. But the walls were too thick. Then they rented the cellar under the House. Here, they stored about 30 barrels of gunpowder.

▷ **The plotters hid the barrels of gunpowder** under piles of firewood. One of them, Guy Fawkes, stayed on guard. He was a fanatical Catholic who had been a captain in the Spanish army.

◁ **Four of the plotters discuss** their plans in Robert Catesby's house in Warwickshire. Catesby is on the left. He was a strong leader, who had already taken part in the Earl of Essex's unsuccessful rebellion against Elizabeth I in 1601.

Eight other men joined in the plot. But this brought disaster. One of the new men had a brother-in-law, Lord Monteagle, who would be in Parliament when the barrels exploded. He sent Monteagle a warning letter in code. Monteagle showed the letter to Robert Cecil, who told the king. So, on the night of 4 November, search parties went to the House. They found the gunpowder and arrested Guy Fawkes. Three days later the rest of the plotters were caught by Cecil's men. Catesby and three others were killed. The remaining eight were put in prison, and executed in 1606.

The failure of the Gunpowder Plot had two important results. It caused people to fear the Catholics even more. And, for a short time, it made Parliament more friendly towards James. After all, few people wanted civil war, and James's heir, Henry, was only 11 years old. MPs made a law naming 5 November as a day of thanksgiving for their narrow escape.

▷ **Robert Cecil**, the chief minister to both Elizabeth I and James I. He was the son of another chief minister, Lord Burghley, and became Earl of Salisbury in 1605. Though frail, he was a clever, patient man who did most of the king's work for him. Cecil died in 1612.

◁ **Guy Fawkes is arrested** by soldiers in the cellar beneath the House of Lords. He was taken to the Tower of London and tortured. But Fawkes refused to give away the names of his friends until he knew the leaders were dead. Two signatures, before and after torture (right), show how badly he suffered. He and the other plotters were hung, drawn and quartered in 1606 (below).

PILGRIMS TO THE NEW WORLD

In 1603, some Puritan clergymen asked the king to allow them to have their own church services. The Puritans were ardent Protestants who wanted greater use of Bible teachings. But James declared that they must use the Church of England service, or he would "harry (chase) them out of the land".

▽ **Pilgrim settlers** trade goods with a local Wampanoag Indian. The first year at Plymouth was very difficult. About half of the settlers died from disease or poor food. Their crops did not grow well. In 1621 they began to get help from the Wampanoag, and made a peace treaty with them.

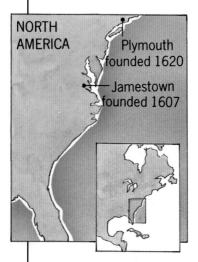

NORTH AMERICA

Plymouth founded 1620

Jamestown founded 1607

△ **The early settlements** in North America. Jamestown and Plymouth were the first to succeed. By 1700, 12 colonies had been set up on the Atlantic coast.

Many Puritans decided to leave Britain and find new homes in North America. There was already one English colony on the Atlantic coast. This was Jamestown, in Virginia, which had been founded in 1607. On 22 December 1620, the ship *Mayflower* reached the coast of what is now called Massachusetts. On board were over 100 Puritans who had broken away from the Church of England. They founded the colony of Plymouth, and are now known as the Pilgrim Fathers.

▷ **An American Indian smoking a pipe of tobacco.** An English colonist, John Rolfe, brought tobacco seeds from South America to Virginia in 1612. Tobacco grew well there, and soon became a valuable crop. Most of it was exported to England.

△ **The Indian village of Secoton**, Virginia, drawn by John White, an English colonist who first came to America in 1585. His picture shows Indian houses, Indians feasting and performing religious ceremonies, and fields planted with corn.

The Pilgrim settlers had to work very hard:
● finding a dry and safe site for their village
● cutting down trees in the nearby forests for timber to build their houses and to clear land to grow crops on
● sowing the seeds they had brought with them
● hoeing the weeds
● hunting for game and fish to eat.

△ **The *Fortune* sails for Plymouth in November 1621. The ship took 35 new settlers to America.**

△ **Turkeys and corn cobs** were sent to Europe from America as new types of food.

The Indians taught the settlers hunting skills and their own ways of growing crops. They showed them how to bury fish in the ground as fertilizer, and how to plant corn, pumpkins and beans.

Thanks to the Indians, the Pilgrims' harvest in autumn 1621 was a very good one. They invited the Wampanoag to a three-day celebration. This festival, called Thanksgiving, has been held by North Americans every year since then.

The Pilgrims lived a simple life, ruled by their Puritan faith. They were not concerned with making money out of trade. As a result, Plymouth did not grow as fast or as rich as other colonies. By 1630, its population was only 300.

By 1700, British colonists were well established and exporting goods to Europe. From the north they sent timber and fish, from the central colonies wheat and other grains, and from the south they sent tobacco and rice. Their numbers had grown to 250,000.

A KING WITHOUT PARLIAMENT

Charles R

James's eldest son, the popular Henry, had died of typhoid in 1612. When James died in 1625, he was succeeded by his second son, Charles. The new king was shy, serious and very religious. He could not make decisions and did not keep his promises.

Actress in court play or 'masque' costume

Charles's reign got off to a bad start. Needing a queen, he quickly married Henrietta Maria, the sister of the king of France. She was a Catholic, and Parliament was alarmed that she might make Charles and their children Catholic too.

Matters were not helped by Buckingham, who was still the king's chief advisor. In 1625 he sent an army to Holland to help fight the Austrian Empire. Later, he began a war with Spain by trying to capture Cadiz harbour. Both expeditions were failures, and many soldiers died. In 1627, Buckingham angered the French by attacking an island near La Rochelle to help Protestants there. The French army drove him off, and he lost 2,000 soldiers. In 1628, Buckingham was stabbed to death by an enraged army officer.

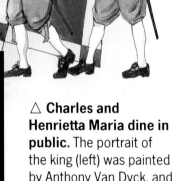

△ **Charles and Henrietta Maria dine in public.** The portrait of the king (left) was painted by Anthony Van Dyck, and shows him on horseback. This disguised the fact that Charles had weak legs.

▷ **William Laud**, who became Archbishop of Canterbury in 1633. He reformed the Church of England and suppressed the Puritans. Many people believed that he was trying to make Britain Catholic again.

Foreign wars were expensive, and Charles was very short of money. He forced rich people to lend him money. Then he asked Parliament to allow him to raise customs duties on wines and many other goods.

But the MPs were angry. They were shocked by the forced loans, the disasters abroad and the behaviour of Buckingham. In 1628, they presented Charles with the Petition of Right, a series of requests. Two of these asked him to stop forced loans and not to imprison people without trial.

Like his father, Charles believed that he ruled by Divine Right, and need take no notice of Parliament. But he wanted money, and agreed to the Petition in 1629. The MPs granted him an increase in customs duties, but only for one year.

Charles would not accept their offer. He decided that he would do without Parliament altogether. On 2 March 1629 he sent royal guards to dismiss the MPs. But when the Speaker (the chairman of the House) tried to stand to announce the closure of Parliament, he was held down by other MPs. The leader of the rebels, Sir John Eliot, read out three resolutions which condemned the king's actions. These were passed. But the Parliament was not to meet again for 11 years.

▷ The *Sovereign of the Seas* was Britain's biggest battleship. Built in 1637, she was paid for by Ship Money, a tax paid by ordinary people for new naval ships.

Since the Middle Ages, only people who lived near the coast had to pay Ship Money. But in 1635 Charles made people from inland areas pay this tax as well. Besides Ship Money, the king had to find other ways of getting money without Parliament. He sold monopolies. A monopoly made the buyer the only person allowed to make or sell certain goods. Charles also fined people who had built on common land, or in the royal forests.

These measures were unpopular. Anyone who refused to pay was tried in special courts. The king was seen as a tyrant.

TROUBLE IN SCOTLAND AND IRELAND

Scotland and Ireland were the poorest parts of the kingdom. Charles had been born in Scotland, but he rarely went there as king. This made him unpopular with the Scots. In 1632, he sent Thomas Wentworth to Ireland as his Lord Deputy. Wentworth ruled so harshly that he was known as Black Tom Tyrant.

▷ **Scottish troops** go to meet the English army at Berwick-on-Tweed in early June 1639, after defeating Scots supporters of the king. Though no battle was fought, it was called the First Bishops' War.

△ **Presbyterians riot** in St Giles's Cathedral in Edinburgh in 1637. The protest, against the forced use of the English Prayer Book, was begun by a woman. She threw her stool at the minister. Soon the rest of the congregation joined in, throwing sticks as well as stools. The riot spread into the city streets.

△ **A Scottish nobleman** presents a petition to the king. This was made by Presbyterian lawyers in 1637. It asked Charles to withdraw his orders about the English Prayer Book. Charles agreed, but it was too late. The Scots were so angry that they began signing the National Covenant instead.

Most Scots were Presbyterians. Their church was stricter than the Protestant Church of England. They had their own prayer book and religious services, and refused to obey Protestant bishops.

In 1637 Charles and Archbishop Laud ordered the Scots to use the new English Prayer Book. The Presbyterians were enraged, and there were riots in church. In 1638, thousands of Scots signed a 'National Covenant', which attacked any change to their religion. The king decided to force them to obey his orders.

An English army arrived at the Scottish border in June 1639. But it was no match for the well-trained Scots soldiers. The king was forced to make peace before a battle was fought. Charles had no money to pay for a bigger army. In despair, he recalled the loyal Wentworth from Ireland, and made him Earl of Strafford. The earl advised Charles to call Parliament and ask for a grant. But the MPs refused to give one. They were sent home after only three weeks. This was known as the Short Parliament.

Meanwhile, unrest was growing in Ireland. Most Irish people were Catholic and hated having a Protestant ruler. They also hated the English and Scottish settlers who had moved into Ulster in the North.

Late in 1641, the Catholic Irish rose in revolt. Led by Phelim O'Neill, they attacked towns and killed more than 3,000 Protestants in Ulster.

Charles, as usual, did not keep his word. He burned the Treaty of Berwick, signed on 19 June 1639, while Strafford put together a new army. But it was no better, and many soldiers refused to fight. In August 1640 the Scots began the Second Bishops' War by marching across the border. They defeated the feeble English army at Newburn and captured New-castle. The king was forced to make peace.

The Treaty of Ripon allowed the Scots to occupy six northern English counties. Worse still, Charles agreed to pay them £850 a day until the dispute was over. This was a huge sum. Once again, the king had to summon Parliament to ask for money. It met in November 1640, and was not dismissed for 20 years. It was called the Long Parliament.

▷ **A portrait of Thomas Wentworth**, drawn in about 1633. While ruling in Ireland, he imposed law and order on disobedient people. He got rid of pirates and bandits, and raised his own small army. He also made sure that taxes were collected, took back lands which belonged to the Crown, and encouraged trade. But he was a ruthless man, and made many enemies.

PARLIAMENT GROWS STRONGER

Charles had tried to rule without Parliament. He had taken great powers for himself. But in the end he had failed because he lacked money. Now the MPs began to take away some of his powers. They refused to grant him taxes until he agreed to their demands.

The first demand was to get rid of the hated Strafford. He was tried for treason, and executed in 1641. Archbishop Laud was imprisoned. The other demands were also met. In a short time, the MPs had abolished the Ship Money tax and the Star Chamber, a court that had been used to punish the king's enemies.

At this moment, in October 1641, there came news of the terrible massacres in Ulster. The king began to assemble an army. But Parliament, led by the Puritan John Pym, was alarmed. The MPs feared Charles would use the army to attack anyone who opposed him in England. Pym demanded that Parliament should decide who led the army. "By God, not for an hour!" replied the angry king.

In November, Pym put before Parliament a long list of what the king had done wrong during his reign. This was called the Grand Remonstrance. It condemned bishops and Catholics and the ministers chosen by Charles. Pym claimed that they should be chosen by Parliament. After long debates, the Remonstrance was passed.

◁ **John Pym**, the leader of the rebels in Parliament. A strict Puritan, he feared that the Catholics were becoming strong again. He also opposed all the king's attempts to be an absolute (all-powerful) monarch. Pym was a fine speaker and a hard worker.

▷ **A huge crowd watches** as the Earl of Strafford is beheaded on Tower Hill, London. He had been brought before Parliament, and found guilty of treason without a fair trial. Charles was forced to sign his death warrant.

A Doctor Vsher, Lord Primate of Ireland,
B the Sherifes of London,
C the Earle of Strafford,
D his kindred and Friends.

Charles now wanted to show Parliament that he ruled the country, not them. He decided to go to the House of Commons and arrest Pym and four rebel MPs for high treason. On 4 January 1642, the king went to Westminster with 400 soldiers. Just before he arrived, the five hunted MPs escaped by boat down the River Thames. Charles marched in and saw he was too late. "All the birds are flown", he said to the Speaker.

Many people were shocked at the king's action. By law, MPs could not be arrested when they were in the House of Commons. Riots broke out in London. A week later, Charles and his family fled from the city.

◁ **The officers who went to Parliament with the king** were called Cavaliers by their enemies. This was an insult. 'Cavalieros' were brutal Catholic troops from Spain. Cavaliers dressed in courtly clothes.

△ **The king and his soldiers** burst into the House of Commons to arrest five rebel MPs. No monarch had ever set foot in the House before. The Speaker (chairman) is about to stand and give Charles his seat. The soldiers bar the exit.

△ **Charles waves farewell to his family from the cliffs of Dover.** Henrietta Maria took her children (and the Crown Jewels) to Holland on 23 February 1642. Civil war now seemed certain, and the king wanted them to be safe. The queen was also going to ask for help and money abroad. Meanwhile, the king moved north to York, and called together his supporters. Parliament also began to train troops. These were called Roundheads because of their short hair.

CIVIL WAR BEGINS

On 22 August 1642, Charles moved south from York to Nottingham. His army was growing, and his nephew Prince Rupert had arrived from Holland to lead the cavalry. But Parliament controlled the main ports, the navy and the city of London.

The king realized that leaving London had been another mistake. So in October he set off for the capital with an army of 13,000 men. The Parliamentary troops, led by the Puritan Earl of Essex, had already left London to cut him off.

The two forces met at Edgehill, near Warwick. Neither side won this first battle, and the king went on towards London. But the city was well defended, and he was forced to withdraw.

CIVIL WAR 1642-43

Marston Moor
Rowton Heath
Nantwich
Naseby
Edgehill
Cropredy
Newbury
Langport
Cheriton
Lostwithiel

▷ **The main battles of the Civil War.** People in the North, Wales and the West mostly supported the king. Those in the South and East mostly supported Parliament.

▽ **A Cavalier and Roundhead** from the Battle of Edgehill. Prince Rupert's cavalry scattered the enemy cavalry at first. But the Parliamentary army fought back bravely. One of their officers was Oliver Cromwell.

Civil War soldiers.
There was no national army at this time. Both sides were made up of local troops raised by noblemen or town councils. This is how they were drawn up in battle:
Pikemen were footsoldiers armed with pointed pikes which were often 4 metres long. They stood in the centre.
Musketeers (one is shown right) were armed with muskets. These guns took a long time to load. Musketeers stood on each side of the pikemen.
Cavalrymen were on horseback and armed with swords and pistols. They rode on either side of the footsoldiers.

Cavalier cavalryman

Roundhead pikeman

Early in 1643, the king set up camp and headquarters in Oxford. For a while everything went his way. Henrietta Maria returned from Holland to join him. Royalists in the West Country captured Bristol and other towns. John Hampden, a Parliamentary leader, was killed in battle. In September, the king signed a truce with the Irish, and brought more troops back to England.

But Pym was working hard to increase his forces. He gained the help of the Scots, who promised to fight the king if Parliament allowed the Presbyterian Church into England.

△ **Sir Thomas Fairfax**, Parliamentarian general

▽ **Prince Rupert's charge** at Edgehill.

△ **Prince Rupert**, the king's nephew. He was only 23 years old when the Civil War began.

Once again, Charles made a bad mistake. Although he had won several battles, he had not advanced on London. He failed to capture the city of Gloucester because he hesitated. Then in September he withdrew from a battle at Newbury that he had almost won.

In January 1644, the Scots came south with 21,000 men and stormed Newcastle. It was now too late for Charles to win.

WINNING THE WAR

"I had rather have a plain russet-coated captain that knows what he fights for, and loves what he knows, than what you call a gentleman, and is nothing else." Oliver Cromwell said this in 1643, about men he wanted in Parliament's army. Soon after, John Pym died, leaving Parliament without an overall leader.

The Scots army, fighting on Parliament's side, changed the war in the north. Three Parliamentary armies besieged York. When Prince Rupert tried to save York for the king, his army was beaten at the Battle of Marston Moor. After this battle, Cromwell was seen as one of Parliament's most important generals. He made sure his men were well trained. York soon fell to Parliament. King Charles had lost northern England.

In the south, Parliament had problems. In September, the Earl of Essex surrendered at Lostwithiel in Cornwall. There were also quarrels about pay and skills between its armies.

▽ **A portrait of Oliver Cromwell**, painted in 1649. Cromwell was a farmer in Cambridgeshire before becoming an MP in the Long Parliament in 1640. He was a strong Puritan and stern leader.

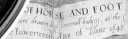

▷ **This print shows how the two armies were drawn up at the Battle of Naseby** in June 1645. The Royalist forces (Cavaliers) are at the top, with the king in the centre and Prince Rupert's cavalry on the left. The Royalist army was only half as big as the enemy's, and had to advance uphill.

◁ **A Roundhead cavalryman**, armed and with protective helmet.

In the winter of 1644-45, Parliament agreed to set up a new army. All the old local armies were broken up and all MPs and Lords gave up their military commands. The 'New Model Army' was made up of 22,000 full-time, paid and trained men. Its commander, Sir Thomas Fairfax, asked Cromwell to be in charge of the cavalry.

The New Model Army met the king's forces at Naseby in Northamptonshire on 14 June 1645. Though Rupert's cavalry had more success, the Royalists were beaten. Charles retreated to the Welsh border. Throughout the rest of the year, his last strongholds, Carlisle, Bristol and Exeter, were lost. By May 1646, the king was under siege at Oxford. He escaped from the city, disguised in a false beard and dark clothes.

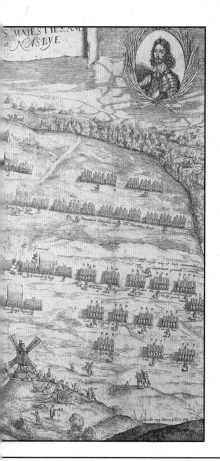

▽ **After Naseby**, the New Model Army went on to defeat another Royalist force at Langport, in Somerset. But in Scotland, Royalist forces under the leadership of the Marquis of Montrose, won victories for King Charles.

Montrose's four victories

Auldean
Alford
Inverlochy
Kilsyth
SCOTLAND
ENGLAND

△ **'Diggers'** at work on common land in Surrey. They believed that land should be shared and not owned just by nobles. Other groups of ordinary people wanted to have the right to vote regularly for MPs. Parliament broke up these groups.

△ **An early meeting of Quakers** (top) in about 1650. The Quakers were a religious group which believed that Christians should live simply. 'Shakers' (above) were another religious group who wanted Parliament to change its ways.

The Civil War really ended in June 1646, when Royalists at Oxford surrendered. The king had given himself up to the Scots, and was trying to get them on his side. Yet his opponents were still arguing with each other about whether or not to increase taxes. Only Cromwell kept the Army and Parliament together.

EXECUTION OF THE KING

"This court doth adjudge that Charles Stuart, as a tyrant, traitor, murderer and public enemy to the good people of this nation, shall be put to death by the severing of his head from his body." This was the sentence of the High Court on Charles I, in 1649.

Charles would not agree to the demands of the Scots, so in February 1647 they handed him over to the English. He was pleased to see that the split between the Parliament and the Army was growing wider. Parliament had ordered the Army to disband, without paying the soldiers.

Cromwell and Fairfax acted quickly. In June they had the king taken to Newmarket, where he would be in the Army's power. Cromwell offered Charles a deal, called the Heads of the Proposals. Parliament would control the Army for ten years, then the king would take command. This was a generous offer, but once again Charles refused. He tried to get help from the Scots a second time. But in November, before the Scots responded, he escaped from house arrest to the Isle of Wight.

Soon a second Civil War had broken out. In 1648, Royalist risings began in Wales and the South. A Scots army crossed the border, this time on the king's side. But one by one, Cromwell and Fairfax crushed them, finally defeating the Scots at Preston.

The king was recaptured and taken to Windsor. The Army leaders now realized that they could not trust him. They declared that Charles must be put on public trial for all his wrongdoings.

But most MPs would not allow such a trial; it seemed wrong to do this to a monarch. So, for the first time, the Army turned against Parliament. On 6 December 1648, Colonel Thomas Pride surrounded the House of Commons with soldiers. All MPs were stopped from going in, except those who wanted a trial. The much smaller Parliament appointed a High Court of 135 people. The trial began on 20 January 1649. A week later, Charles I was sentenced to death.

△ **John Bradshaw**, the President of the High Court which tried Charles. He wore a special hat (above) lined with steel to protect him from the king's supporters.

△ **The king in court.** Charles refused to defend himself against the charges. He said that the High Court was illegal. Many people, including Thomas Fairfax, agreed.

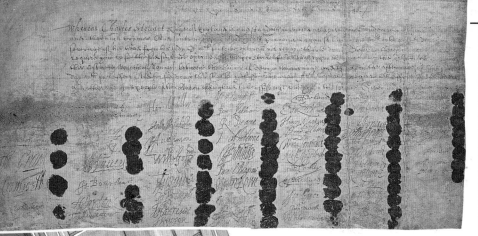

△ **The king's death warrant**, signed by the judges. Cromwell's signature is on the left.

▷ **The morning of 30 January 1649** was very cold. Charles asked his servant for a second shirt in case people saw him shivering and thought he was afraid. "I fear not death" he said. He walked calmly to the Banqueting Hall at the Palace of Whitehall. At one o'clock he stepped through an open window and onto the wooden scaffold that had been built outside.

△ **The execution official holds up the head of the king.** Before he died, Charles had been allowed to make a speech to the large and silent crowd below. He told them, "I am a martyr of the people". Then he knelt at the block and his head was cut off with one blow of the axe. One man yelled, "This is the head of a traitor!" But many of the crowd groaned.

ENGLAND WITHOUT A KING

Charles I was dead, and Britain was now a Republic, or Commonwealth. This meant that it was not ruled by a monarch. However, no one knew how the country should be governed. Oliver Cromwell was now the most powerful person in the country.

"Irish Homeland"

△ **Ireland after Cromwell's expedition in 1650.** He took land from Catholics and gave it to English Protestant settlers. The rebels found safety only in the Connacht region.

◁ **Cromwell's army** storms the town of Drogheda, Ireland, in 1649. The citizens refused to surrender, and when Cromwell's forces finally broke in, they massacred more than 2,600 people.

First of all, Cromwell faced threats of invasion from Ireland and Scotland. The Irish Catholics were shocked at Charles's execution, and rose to support the Royalists. In September 1649, Cromwell arrived in Ireland with the New Model Army to crush the rebels. His troops killed thousands of Catholics.

In June 1650, Cromwell had to dash to Scotland. The dead king's son, Charles II, was leading an army which was about to invade England. Though defeated at Dunbar, the Royalist army marched on south. It was not until September 1651 that Cromwell finally destroyed the Scots at Worcester. Charles II fled to France.

Cromwell and the Army had made the Republic safe. But they thought that the government was unfair. After quarrels with the remaining MPs, Cromwell closed Parliament in April 1653. Later that year, a Parliament was created that was made up of 140 godly (religious) men, chosen from the independent churches. People mockingly called it Barebone's Parliament, after one of the members, Praisegod Barebone. It suggested changes to the laws and Church that were impractical. The Army commanders decided that Cromwell should be head of the government in their place.

▽ **Very few people in this crowd** were actually allowed to take part in a General Election. Under Cromwell's rule, only those who owned property worth £200 could vote. This made Cromwell unpopular with ordinary people, who were also unhappy that the Army was involved in government.

◁ **An election for Parliament** takes place in an English village. The local officer shows the crowd the list of candidates. During the rule of the Major-Generals, from 1655 to 1657, these officers toured the country telling people to vote for MPs who were Puritans.

△ **The death mask of Oliver Cromwell**, made from a wax impression. Cromwell's various experiments in governing Britain failed. Parliament offered him the Crown more than once, but he refused. After his death, his son Richard became Lord Protector, but for only a year.

Cromwell was appointed Lord Protector in December 1653. He was to rule with a Council of State and a new Parliament. One of the first things he did was make a peace treaty with the Dutch, in 1654. This ended years of trade wars between the two countries and helped expand the British overseas empire. But Cromwell did not get on well with Parliament, or with the rule by 11 Puritan Major-Generals that followed. In 1657 he took control again, but he died a year later.

25

CHARLES II 1660 – 1685

At the beginning of 1660, Britain had no head of state. There was the danger of another civil war. But George Monck, an Army general, now made a popular decision. He invited Charles II to return to England and become king. On 25 May 1660, Charles landed in Kent and rode to London.

Charles wanted to be a strong king, but he could not stop Royalist revenge on the Puritans. His chief minister, Lord Clarendon, passed new laws stating that Puritans could not have government jobs, and would be fined if they held their own kinds of church service.

The king tried to increase British power in Europe by making a secret treaty with France in 1670. He wanted help in a war against Holland. In exchange, he promised freedom for Catholics to worship.

▷ **Charles at a court ball.** His queen was Catherine of Braganza, a Portuguese princess. They had married in 1662 to seal an alliance between Britain and Portugal. The queen had no children, and was often ignored by the king. He had many mistresses, including the actress Nell Gwynn, and enjoyed dancing and horse-racing. Charles died in 1685 after a short illness.

▷ **The Royal Gardener** hands a pineapple to the king. It was the first pineapple grown in England. Charles encouraged many new scientific ideas.

▽ **A coin, touched by the king**, was believed to protect against disease.

Many MPs were furious when they found out about the king's treaty with France. Most of them still hated Catholics, especially the powerful French King Louis XIV. In 1673, Parliament passed the Test Act. This forced all public officials to swear that they were Protestants. Yet Charles's brother James was a Catholic, as well as heir to the throne.

The king's main opponent was the Earl of Shaftesbury. His supporters became known as the Whigs. Other MPs, who supported Charles, were called the Tories. Matters grew worse in 1678, when James was accused of plotting to murder the king and take his throne. This was a lie, but alarming.

Catholics were beaten up in the streets. Shaftesbury tried to pass a law preventing James from becoming the next king. But in 1681 Louis XIV gave Charles a huge sum of money. Now Charles no longer had to depend on taxes from Parliament. He went to Westminster and dismissed the MPs. The crisis ended.

◁ **Court ladies** in the grand dresses which were now fashionable. After the drab years under Puritan rule, people had fun again. Theatres, which had been closed, opened.

▽ **Men gossip, smoke and drink black coffee** in a coffee house. These became popular in London during Charles's reign. They grew into meeting places for groups of all kinds, including plotters against the king. In 1675, Parliament even tried to close them down, but was unsuccessful.

PLAGUE AND FIRE

"Lord, how empty the streets are, and melancholy, so many poor sick people in the streets, full of sores, and so many sad stories overheard as I walk, everybody talking of this man dead, and that man sick." So wrote Samuel Pepys in 1665. Two disasters struck London at the beginning of Charles II's reign: the plague of 1665 and the Great Fire of 1666.

Rat and plague flea

The plague broke out in the spring of 1665. It was bubonic plague, which had also killed many people during the Middle Ages. The disease was spread by fleas carried by rats. There was no cure, and it swiftly spread through the crowded and dirty London streets.

At night, men drove carts through the streets, shouting "Bring out your dead!" The corpses were collected and buried in huge 'plague pits' at the edge of the City. Altogether, nearly 100,000 Londoners died during this outbreak. Puritans believed that the plague was God's punishment for Charles's wicked ways.

On 2 September 1666, a fire started in a bakery in Pudding Lane. A spark lit a pile of hay in a nearby inn yard. The flames swept into warehouses full of oil and candle wax. By the morning, the blaze was out of control.

The fire raged for five days, covering most of the City. Nine people died, and more than 13,000 houses and 97 churches were destroyed, including St Paul's Cathedral. Afterwards, Sir Christopher Wren drew up plans for new buildings. But only part of his scheme was adopted, including the new St Paul's, which stands today, with its huge dome.

How Londoners tried to deal with the plague:
● Bonfires were burned in the streets to purify the air. The dead were buried quickly (see above, from a print of the time).
● Many people, including the king and his court, fled to the country.
● Doctors wore leather coats, gloves and masks stuffed with herbs to ward off the disease.
● Infected houses were shut up and marked with a cross. The people inside were left to die.

◁ **Samuel Pepys**, a navy clerk who kept a diary between 1660 and 1669. This gives a lively picture of London life, and describes both the plague and the Great Fire.

▽ **Samuel Pepys and a friend watch the fire from the top of Barking Church.** They can see:
● old St Paul's Cathedral blazing in the distance. Molten lead poured from its roof
● householders loading their goods and furniture into carts to drive them away to safety
● men pulling the straw thatch from the roofs to stop it catching fire
● fire-fighters about to douse the flames with water pumped from the Thames
● people escaping from burning buildings. Many narrow streets were blocked.

The fire was finally stopped by filling some houses with gunpowder and blowing them up. This made a gap in the street that was too wide for the fire to cross.

JAMES II 1685 – 1688

"This good prince (James II) has all the weakness of his father without his strength … and he is as very a Papist (Catholic) as the Pope himself, which will be his ruin." – said by the Earl of Lauderdale in 1679. James II became king in 1685. England had its first openly Catholic king since Henry VIII.

James began his reign in a strong position. He had a standing army. His enemies in Parliament, the Whigs, had been beaten and many had gone abroad. Parliament was controlled by the Tories, who granted the king much more money in taxes.

But James was a stupid man. He wanted Britain to become a Catholic country again. The Whigs did not trust him. They planned to replace him with the Duke of Monmouth, a bastard son of Charles II. In June 1685, Monmouth led a rebel army into Somerset. But his untrained force was quickly crushed by James's troops at the Battle of Sedgemoor.

▽ **A portrait of Judge George Jeffreys.** In autumn 1685, in courts in Dorchester, Exeter and Bristol, he tried members of Monmouth's rebellion. He savagely sentenced more than 300 of them to death, including Monmouth. Jeffreys showed no mercy, and the trials became known as The Bloody Assize. The judge later became Lord Chancellor.

◁ **A painting of James II in 1685.** The ship in the background shows that the king had been Chief Admiral of the navy. On the left is the king's crown.

▷ **James flees from London** by boat in mid-December 1688. Here his boat passes under London Bridge at the dead of night. His first attempt to escape England was unsuccessful. But he made it the second time, on 24 December. James died in 1701.

Now the king started to increase the power of the Catholics. They were made officers in the army, and given government jobs. In April 1687, James issued his 'Declaration of Indulgence'. This would get rid of many of the laws against Catholics. When Parliament refused to pass it, he dismissed them. In May 1688, James commanded that his Declaration should be read out in every church. Seven bishops who refused to do this were arrested. They were tried, but found not guilty. Yet Protestant anger was high. William III of Holland was invited to be king. Later that year, James fled to France.

After the release of the seven bishops, leading Whigs and Tories invited William of Orange, a Protestant, to be king of England. William was already ruler of Holland, but he was married to Mary Stuart, one of James's two daughters, who were Protestant.

◁ **William of Orange lands at Torbay**, Devon, on 5 November 1688. He brought with him a well-trained army of 15,000 men. As William's forces headed towards London, people in towns along his way declared their support for him. William spoke only of wanting to halt James's plan of making the country Roman Catholic again. But he ended up becoming monarch. William's invasion was later called The Glorious Revolution since no blood was shed.

THE LATER STUARTS 1688–1714

William III and Mary II were crowned on 11 April 1689. Parliament allowed them to rule together. In return, the king and queen agreed to a 'Declaration of Rights'. This gave more power to Parliament, and prevented any Catholic from being monarch.

▷ **The new St Paul's Cathedral** being built in London. It was started in 1675, and took 36 years to finish.

△ **A plate showing William and Mary** at their coronation. Both were Protestants. Although they were joint rulers of Britain, Mary allowed her husband to make most decisions about how to run the country.

William was not popular. He seemed unfriendly. His main interest was in his struggle with France. As ruler of Holland, he had fought many battles to stop the French from invading his country. In early 1689, French troops joined the Catholics in Ireland to support James II. William defeated them at the Battle of the Boyne in 1690.

△ **Jonathan Swift** wrote many pamphlets and books. His most famous work is the story of *Gulliver's Travels*.

△ **John Dryden** was a poet and playwright. In James II's time he became a Catholic. This made him unpopular with William III.

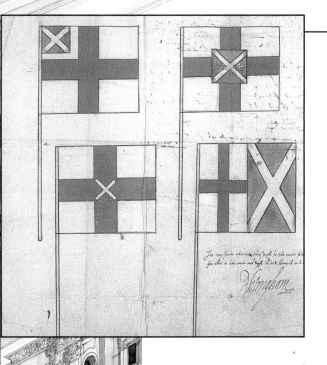

◁ **Designs for a flag** combining the crosses of St George for England (red) and St Andrew for Scotland (white on blue background). In May 1707, the English and Scottish Parliaments were replaced by a new Parliament of Great Britain. This contained 45 Scottish MPs and 513 English and Welsh MPs. Scotland kept its own legal system, schools and Presbyterian Church.

William's victory at the Boyne meant that Ulster would remain a Protestant region in Ireland. Even today, many Irish Protestants still call themselves 'Orangemen' after William.

Mary died in 1694. William remained as king. In 1702, he fell from his horse when it stumbled on a molehill. He broke his collarbone and later died. Because he had no children, Mary's sister Anne became the new queen.

Anne was the first monarch to rule over the United Kingdom of Great Britain, after Scotland united with England and Wales in 1707. She was also the last of the Stuarts to reign. Plump and plain, she was never healthy. Although she gave birth to six children, they all died very young.

At first, Anne relied on advice from her favourite, Sarah Churchill, the wife of the Duke of Marlborough. Most of the daily work of government was done by Sidney Godolphin and Robert Harley. In 1709, the queen quarrelled with the Marlboroughs, and Harley swiftly became her most powerful minister.

△ **Christopher Wren** helped to rebuild London after the Great Fire. He designed many churches and hospitals.

△ **Isaac Newton** was one of the greatest of all scientists. He made the first mirror telescope, and studied gravity.

PEOPLE AND THEIR HOMES

The population of Britain grew steadily during the 17th century. The number of people rose from 6.7 million to about 9.25 million. But each year many still died of disease, especially during the plague year of 1665. And only one baby in four lived to be an adult.

▷ **A Stuart town house.** After the Great Fire, Charles II proclaimed that all new town buildings should be made of brick and stone.

By 1700 there were more big towns in England than ever before. Older cities such as Norwich and Bristol were being matched by new ports like Liverpool and centres of industry like Leeds and Nottingham. London was by far the biggest city, and more than half a million people lived there.

However, most Britons still lived in the countryside. Very few owned their own homes or land. They rented houses from the local landowner, and probably worked for him too. The houses were small and made of local materials. About 160 English noblemen owned more than

one-fifth of all the land, and their estates were getting bigger. Very wealthy men like that could afford to build grand new houses. Between 1690 and 1714 many big country houses were built, including Castle Howard in Yorkshire and Chatsworth House in Derbyshire. Grandest of all was Blenheim Palace in Oxfordshire, which was built as a gift for the Duke of Marlborough in 1705.

High-quality furniture became grander and more comfortable. Wooden beds and mantels were carved with rich designs. For the first time, chairs were upholstered (padded and covered).

▷ **A supper party at an inn** in about 1610. In 1603 there were nearly 20,000 inns in England and Wales. Some were large taverns built beside the main coach roads. Coach passengers stopped to eat or to stay the night. Coaching inns could house 300 guests. Other inns were simple alehouses, where local people went to drink. In 1604, James I ordered that only travellers could be served at an inn. Locals could only drink there for one hour at midday.

▽ **A coach passes the house.** It is pulled by horses, but the sedan chair next to it is carried by two men. Sedan chairs developed from horse-drawn chairs called litters.

◁ **A town house** belonging to a wealthy middle class family in about 1700. It is 'double pile' (two rooms deep) and has four floors. In the basement at the back are the kitchen and scullery where the servants work. The family lives and eats in rooms on the ground floor. Above that are the bedrooms and attic.

◁ **The house has plain brick walls**, but there are decorations above the entrance and along the eaves of the roof. The windows are much bigger than in earlier times, and have two sliding parts. Iron railings and a gate separate the front of the house from the street.

TRADE AND TRANSPORT

During the 1670s, British trade began to grow very quickly. Europeans had founded settlements and trading stations in many parts of the world. More goods than ever were coming into British ports, especially London, Bristol and Liverpool. More goods were also being made by Britain's new industries.

▽ **Some ways in which goods and people were carried on land:**
● by packhorse
● by cart. Big carriers' carts took cargoes and mail regularly between towns.
● by coach. Stage coaches could take passengers up to 80 kilometres a day. Horses were changed at every 'stage' of the journey.

▽ **A coastal port.** A cargo boat carries goods upriver to a larger port, where they will be loaded into ocean-going ships.

Road travel in Stuart times was slowed by muddy, rutted highways.
● In 1663, the first toll roads were opened. Carriers had to pay to use them. The money was used to repair the roads.
● To keep their feet clear of the mud and dirt, people generally wore tall pattens (thick wooden soles) held on with straps and buckles.

◁ The busy port of Bristol at the beginning of the 18th century. Ships brought sugar, tobacco and cotton, and carried away British goods such as cloth and cast iron.

▽ An English family 'taking tea'. By 1700, tea was a fashionable drink. It was served without milk in Chinese cups and saucers.

Most British people worked on the land, as they had done since the Middle Ages. Ways of farming had changed little.

But there were greater changes in industry. A new kind of windmill, the smock mill, was built. Unlike earlier mills, which turned with the wind, this had a fixed base. Only the upper part holding the 'sails' moved. Smock mills pumped water and powered timber saws, as well as grinding corn.

Britain was rich in coal and iron. For centuries iron had been extracted from ore by melting it in furnaces. The furnaces used charcoal (made from wood) as their fuel. But by 1700 the supply of trees for charcoal was running out. In 1709, Abraham Darby of Shropshire began to use coke (baked coal) instead. Soon, many new coal mines were being dug.

Besides iron, many other important goods were being made or prepared in Britain and sold abroad. From Scotland came meat, salt and linen. From England came blown glass, leather, wheat, paper, stone, rope, metal tools and equipment, and cloth made from wool and silk.

Britain also became a centre of world trade. British merchants brought in goods from many lands, then sold them on again to people in Europe. Huge catches of fish came from the North Atlantic, and furs from the forests of North America. Silk thread, cotton cloth and costly spices were brought from India and the Far East. New kinds of food also arrived. Sugar from the Caribbean was used instead of honey to sweeten dishes. Coffee and cocoa from South America, and tea from India, became popular drinks. Potatoes from America began to be widely grown.

SLAVE TRADE AND EMPIRE

By 1600, explorers from Europe had set up sea routes to many parts of the world. The Portuguese had trading stations in India. The Dutch were in Malaysia and North America. The French were in Canada. Now Britain began to build up her own trading empire. Within 200 years it would be the biggest in the world.

△ **Chains worn by slaves** who were shipped from Africa to the West Indies. Thousands of slaves died on the voyage.

The English East India Company was founded in 1600. By 1613, it had opened its first trading station in Surat, on the west coast of India. The company brought saltpetre (to make gunpowder), dyes and cotton cloth back to England. By 1647 it had 23 trading stations.

In North America, the Hudson's Bay Company began trading furs in 1670. Traders bought beaver skins from local Indians in exchange for guns and knives. Meanwhile, more colonies were founded on the Atlantic coast, including Carolina and Pennsylvania. In 1664, British troops seized the Dutch town, New Amsterdam. It was given a new name: New York.

But most wealth came from the West Indies. There was a huge demand for sugar, so many more plantations were started. By 1670, the British controlled most of the sugar trade. However, most of the local people had died because of disease and bad treatment. More workers were needed.

So, during the 17th century, the slave trade grew up. British traders had a triangular sea route. They sailed to West Africa, where they exchanged cloth, guns and salt for black slaves. The slaves were taken to the West Indies, and exchanged for sugar, which was then carried back to England.

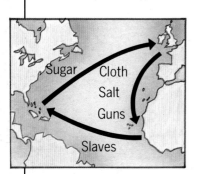

△ **The sea routes used by slave traders.** In 1700, a slave could be sold in the Caribbean for £25 to work on a sugar plantation (right).

How Britain's empire grew:
1600 East India Company formed.
1620 Pilgrim Fathers land at New Plymouth.
1655 Jamaica captured from Spain.
1664 New Amsterdam captured from the Dutch.
1670 Hudson's Bay Company formed.
1672 Royal Africa Company formed.
1683 Pennsylvania founded in North America.

△ **The English fleet** destroys Dutch ships in the North Sea in 1653 to control its trade routes.

▷ **A cargo ship being built** in the East India Company's dockyard at Deptford on the River Thames. The ship is called an East Indiaman, and will be used to bring cloth, spices and other goods from India and the Far East. It can carry about 360 tonnes of cargo, and also has guns to defend itself against attacks by pirates and enemy ships.

MARLBOROUGH AND WAR

For most of the Stuart Age, Britain kept out of wars in Europe. But when William became king in 1689, he was already at war with France. The French, under Louis XIV, were trying to invade Holland and other parts of Europe to expand their empire. William wanted to use Britain's army against Louis.

In 1700, the king of Spain died, and left his throne to Philip, a grandson of Louis. William and other monarchs feared that France would now take over the large Spanish empire, which included Sardinia, Sicily and colonies in North America. So, during 1701, a Grand Alliance was formed to fight the French. It included England, Scotland, Holland, Austria and Prussia. It aimed to make the Archduke of Austria king of Spain instead of Philip. The war was called the War of the Spanish Succession.

William had prepared carefully for this struggle. He had built up a strong British army, using many tough Dutch soldiers. He also had a powerful navy. But in 1702 he died before he could lead them into war. His place as military commander was taken by the Duke of Marlborough.

△ **Queen Anne**, who came to the throne in 1702, just before the War of the Spanish Succession broke out. Her closest friend was Sarah Churchill, the clever and beautiful wife of the Duke of Marlborough. Sarah was a powerful figure at court.

▷ **Workmen are filling in a window space** with bricks so that the house will have fewer windows. In 1692, Parliament imposed a Window Tax on homes with seven or more windows. Many people blocked up windows to avoid it. From 1702, the tax was used to pay for the war.

The French began the war by marching on Vienna, Austria, in 1702. Next year, they were joined by Bavarian forces (from Germany). In a bold attack, Marlborough advanced his troops from the North Sea coast right into Germany. In 1704 he defeated the French and Bavarians at the Battle of Blenheim.

The French had been beaten, and Marlborough returned home a hero. But the war was not over yet. In 1706, Marlborough defeated the French again at Ramillies, near Brussels. He won two more victories, at Oudenarde in 1708 and Malplaquet in 1709.

By now, the British had grown tired of the war. At Malplaquet, the Alliance forces had lost 24,000 men. In 1713, both sides made peace with the Treaty of Utrecht. Marlborough was no longer the army leader. He had been dismissed from his government jobs in 1711, after the queen had argued with his wife.

△ **A view of the Battle of Blenheim**, fought on 2 August 1704. The Duke of Marlborough had marched his troops into Germany to join Austrian forces. They met a much stronger French and Bavarian army near Blindheim (in English, Blenheim) on the River Danube. Marlborough's cavalry broke through the enemy lines and drove them into the river.

▽ **Blenheim Palace** in Oxfordshire as it looks today. It was designed by the playwright and architect Sir John Vanbrugh and took 13 years to build. It was a gift from the queen to Marlborough for his victory at Blenheim.

◁ **John Churchill** became one of King William's leading generals. But the king did not trust him, and imprisoned him in 1692. When war came in 1702, Churchill returned to favour and was made Duke of Marlborough by Queen Anne. He was a brilliant military leader.

SCIENTIFIC DISCOVERIES

"I seem to have been only like a boy playing on the seashore, and diverting myself in now and then finding a smoother pebble or a prettier shell than ordinary, whilst the great ocean of truth lay all undiscovered before me." Isaac Newton said this to compare his discoveries with what was still unknown.

The 17th century saw many great steps forward in science. In 1626, the scholar Francis Bacon caught his death of cold while trying to stuff a chicken with ice. He was trying to discover whether ice would preserve meat. In 1628, William Harvey showed how blood circulates through the body. And in 1660 the Irish scientist Robert Boyle showed that the pressure of gases increases as they are compressed (squeezed), leading to the invention of air pumps.

Charles II wanted to encourage scientists, so in 1662 he helped to found the Royal Society in London. It still exists today.

▷ **The first lighthouse** on the dangerous Eddystone Rock, off the coast of Cornwall. Henry Winstanley began building it in 1694 to warn ships away from the rock. He sunk iron bars in the rock and put a stone and wood tower on top. The light itself burned 26 candles. The lighthouse was swept away in a storm in 1703, with Winstanley inside it.

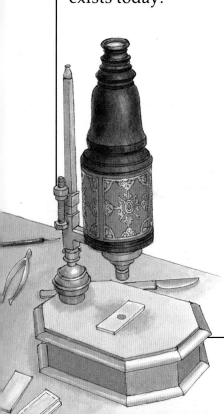

◁ **A microscope** made in London in 1700 after a design by physicist Robert Hooke. It was used to examine many tiny living things, including fleas.

▷ **The Octagonal Room** of the Royal Observatory at Greenwich, London. The Observatory was built by Christopher Wren in 1675. Here, a list was made of over 300 fixed stars to help sailors navigate.

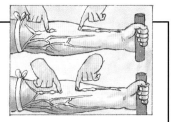

△ **A picture based on William Harvey's book** about the circulation of the blood. It shows how blood in the veins and arteries of the arm can only flow in one direction.

▽ **Doctors** were at last allowed by the Church to cut up dead bodies to study anatomy.

△ **Robert Boyle** with his air pump. Inside the glass jar is a rat. Boyle showed that by using his pump, the air was drawn out of the jar; the rat developed difficulty in breathing.

△ **A steam engine** invented by Thomas Newcomen in about 1705, as drawn at the time. It pumped flood water from coal mines.

▷ **Jethro Tull** with the seed drill he invented in about 1701. Before this, seed was scattered about the fields by hand. Much was wasted, or eaten by birds. The drill sowed seed into the soil in rows.

In 1675, Charles also set up the Royal Observatory at Greenwich. Here, John Flamsteed spent 40 years making a catalogue of the stars. At the same time, Edmund Halley watched comets, and worked out when the next 'great comet' would appear. We call it Halley's Comet.

These men were helped by the greatest scientist of the age, Sir Isaac Newton. One of his earliest inventions was the reflecting telescope of 1668. This used mirrors instead of lenses to magnify what was being looked at. But Newton is best known for his great discoveries about gravity and light. When he was only 23, he realized that objects are pulled towards the Earth by the force of gravity. The same force keeps the Moon in orbit around the Earth. His theory was not published until 1687. Newton also performed experiments to show that sunlight is made of many separate colours.

Meanwhile, a new kind of power was being developed. In 1698, Thomas Savery built a steam pump for draining mines. It was later improved by Thomas Newcomen. The age of steam had begun.

FAMOUS PEOPLE OF STUART TIMES

Robert Cecil, 1563?-1612, followed his father as advisor to Elizabeth I and, when she died, advised James I (see page 7, 8).

Robert Cecil

Sarah Churchill, 1660-1744, was a childhood friend of Queen Anne, and the wife of John Churchill, Duke of Marlborough. She was given a lot of power and land, but quarrelled with Anne over the Queen's friendship with another lady at court, Abigail Masham.

Oliver Cromwell, 1599-1658, was a Parliamentarian general. He became Lord Protector after the Civil War, but believed that Parliament should run the country (see pages 24, 25).

Daniel Defoe, 1661?-1731, was an author. His most famous book is *Robinson Crusoe* but he also wrote a history of pirates and piracy.

John Eliot, 1592-1632, was one of the most outspoken opponents of James I in Parliament (see page 13).

Guy Fawkes, 1570-1606, was caught and executed for his part in the Gunpowder Plot (see pages 8, 9).

Margaret Fell, 1614-1702, was a Quaker who helped organize Quakers in the north of England. Both she and George Fox, the founder of the Quakers, were sent to prison many times for their beliefs.

Nell Gwynn, 1650-87, was Charles II's most famous mistress (see page 26).

Nell Gwynn

Thomas Hobbes, 1588-1679, was one of many people in Stuart times to write a book about how countries should be governed. His book, *Leviathan*, one of the most famous, was published in 1651.

George Jeffreys, 1648-89, was a lawyer who became most famous for his part in the trials of the Monmouth rebels (see page 30).

Inigo Jones, 1573-1652, was an architect and the surveyor of the king's works under Charles I. He designed many Stuart buildings, including parts of Covent Garden and the Banqueting Hall at Westminster, both in London.

William Laud, 1573-1645, was Archbishop of Canterbury. He was accused of treason by Parliament in 1640, imprisoned in the Tower of London in 1641 and executed in 1645 (see page 13).

John Lilburne, 1614-57, was a leader of the Levellers, a group which wanted England to be a Republic (with no monarch). He was sent to prison for his ideas.

James, Duke of Monmouth, 1649-85, was the son of Charles II and his mistress. Because he was illegitimate, he could not become king. But in 1685, Monmouth led a rebellion against the Catholic James II (see page 30).

Thomas Newcomen, 1663-1729, was the inventor of the steam engine. He adapted the design of a steam pump used for getting the water out of mines, which had been invented by Thomas Savery.

Isaac Newton, 1642-1727, was a scientist who wrote books on mathematics, astronomy and other science subjects (see page 33).

Samuel Pepys, 1633-1703, worked for the Navy Office in London, and kept a diary which tells us a lot about life in London at the time (see pages 28, 29).

Pocahontas, 1595-1617, was the daughter of an American Indian chief who is supposed to have saved a British settler, John Smith, from being killed by her tribe. She married a settler called John Rolfe and came back to England with him.

John Pym, 1584-1643, was a Puritan MP who led protests against Charles I (see pages 18, 19).

Prince Rupert, 1619-1682, was Charles I's nephew. He fought for Charles in the Civil Wars (see pages 18, 19).

Jethro Tull, 1647-1741, was a landowner who invented a seed drill for sowing seeds (see page 42).

George Villiers, 1592-1628, the Duke of Buckingham, was chief advisor to James I and Charles I (see page 6).

George Villiers

George Walker, 1618-90, was a clergyman in Derry who raised Protestant soldiers to fight James II in 1688-89. They captured Derry and were besieged there, living on rats and grass, before they had to surrender. Walker was killed at the Battle of the Boyne.

Thomas Wentworth, 1593-1641, was the Earl of Strafford. He governed the north of England and Ireland for Charles I (see page 15).

Christopher Wren, 1632-1723, was a scientist and architect. His most famous building is St Paul's Cathedral (see page 33).

THE ROYAL STUARTS FAMILY TREE

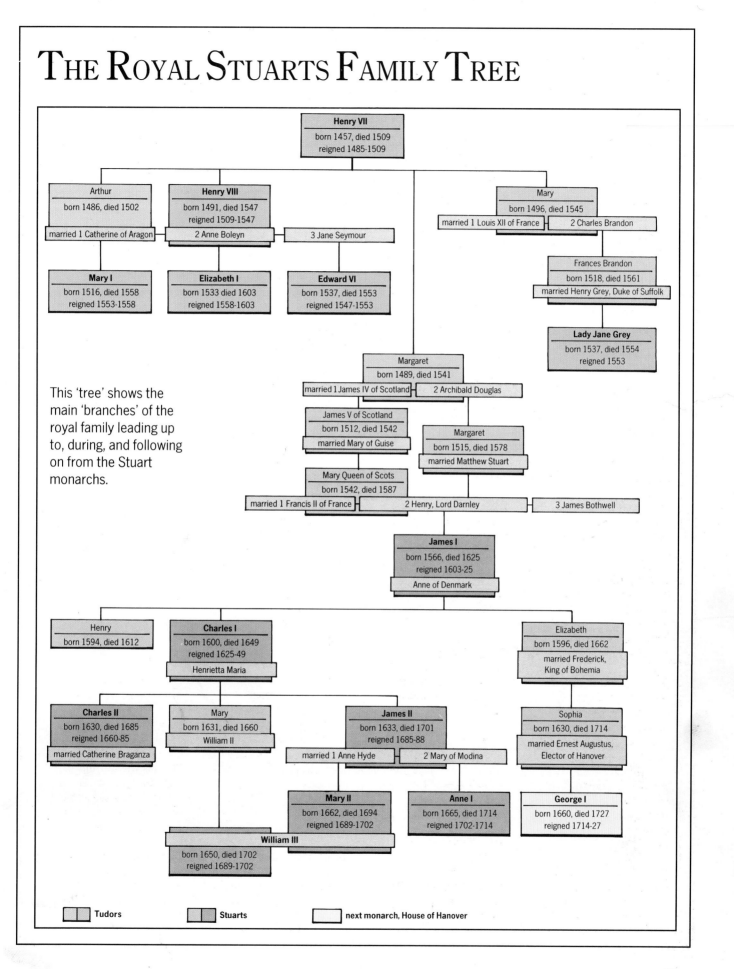

This 'tree' shows the main 'branches' of the royal family leading up to, during, and following on from the Stuart monarchs.

Henry VII
born 1457, died 1509
reigned 1485-1509

Arthur
born 1486, died 1502
married 1 Catherine of Aragon

Henry VIII
born 1491, died 1547
reigned 1509-1547
2 Anne Boleyn

3 Jane Seymour

Mary
born 1496, died 1545
married 1 Louis XII of France 2 Charles Brandon

Mary I
born 1516, died 1558
reigned 1553-1558

Elizabeth I
born 1533 died 1603
reigned 1558-1603

Edward VI
born 1537, died 1553
reigned 1547-1553

Frances Brandon
born 1518, died 1561
married Henry Grey, Duke of Suffolk

Lady Jane Grey
born 1537, died 1554
reigned 1553

Margaret
born 1489, died 1541
married 1 James IV of Scotland 2 Archibald Douglas

James V of Scotland
born 1512, died 1542
married Mary of Guise

Margaret
born 1515, died 1578
married Matthew Stuart

Mary Queen of Scots
born 1542, died 1587
married 1 Francis II of France 2 Henry, Lord Darnley 3 James Bothwell

James I
born 1566, died 1625
reigned 1603-25
Anne of Denmark

Henry
born 1594, died 1612

Charles I
born 1600, died 1649
reigned 1625-49
Henrietta Maria

Elizabeth
born 1596, died 1662
married Frederick, King of Bohemia

Charles II
born 1630, died 1685
reigned 1660-85
married Catherine Braganza

Mary
born 1631, died 1660
William II

James II
born 1633, died 1701
reigned 1685-88
married 1 Anne Hyde 2 Mary of Modina

Sophia
born 1630, died 1714
married Ernest Augustus, Elector of Hanover

Mary II
born 1662, died 1694
reigned 1689-1702

Anne I
born 1665, died 1714
reigned 1702-1714

George I
born 1660, died 1727
reigned 1714-27

William III
born 1650, died 1702
reigned 1689-1702

Tudors   Stuarts   next monarch, House of Hanover

45

GLOSSARY

alliance an agreement to work or fight together.

banish to send a person out of the country and forbid their return.

banquet a grand meal, with lots of fine food.

bastard a person whose parents are not married.

Catholics (Roman Catholics) Christians who follow the religious guidance of the Pope (in Rome).

City the city of London.

civil war a war fought between several groups of people in the same country.

colonies land belonging to a country elsewhere. In Stuart times, there were French, English and Dutch colonies in North America.

Commonwealth country, or countries, effectively ruled by Parliament and not by a monarch.

courtier someone who was part of the monarch's court and usually lived with the monarch.

customs duty a tax paid on goods brought into the country.

disband, dissolve break up.

Divine Right the right to rule believed to be given by God.

government the people who run the country: the monarch, his Privy Council, Parliament and local government officials, such as Justices of the Peace.

harry to repeatedly punish or attack a person or group.

heir person who receives someone's possessions when they die, including the right to become the next king or queen.

household people who live with and work for the owner of the house.

Lord Chancellor one of the king's most important advisors, responsible for the law courts.

monarch king or queen.

monopoly the right to be the only person to sell or make something.

Parliament the House of Lords (nobles and important churchmen) and the House of Commons (gentlemen elected by gentlemen) meeting to advise the king. Only the monarch could call Parliament, and no women or people below the class of gentry could vote on who was in the Commons.

penalties punishments.

persecution unjustly punishing people for their beliefs or their nationality.

petition a written request for something from someone with power.

Presbyterian a strict type of Protestant church.

Protestant part of the Christian church that separated from the Roman Catholic church in the 16th century.

Puritans Christians who wanted greater emphasis on bible teachings and readings and less formal or 'priestly' churches and church services.

rebellion an uprising against the people running the country, to try to replace them.

Republic a country ruled by a group of officials elected by the people.

resolution a decision to do or not do something like pass a law, usually made by a group of MPs.

standing army an army which is permanent, paid and ready to go to war at any time.

suppress to stop a thing happening, or to stop people behaving in a particular way.

tallow melted animal fat, usually used to make candles.

title names, often with land and money attached to it, which the monarch could give away – for example, Duke of Buckingham.

Places to Visit

Here are some Stuart sites or museums of Stuart interest to visit. Your local Tourist Office will be able to tell you about places in your area.

Ardress House, Portadown, Northern Ireland A 17th-century farmhouse with a display of farm tools.

The Banqueting House, Whitehall, London Designed by Inigo Jones.

Blenheim Palace, Woodstock, Oxfordshire Home of John Churchill, Duke of Marlborough. Good for family history and Stuart building styles.

Burghley House, Cambridgeshire The Cecil family lived here. Good for buildings, daily life and the Cecils.

Carisbrooke Castle, Isle of Wight Charles I was imprisoned here before his trial, and tried to escape.

Chatsworth House, Derbyshire Fine example of Stuart architecture and furnishings. Also has a large collection of Inigo Jones designs.

Church of St. Chads, Farndon, Cheshire Famous stained glass window showing Civil War dress.

Church of St. Charles the Martyr, Tunbridge Wells Good Restoration interior.

Coppinger's Court, Ross Carberry, Eire A 17th-century 'strong' or fortified house.

Erddig, Wrexham, Wales Late-Stuart house with many original features, including kitchen, laundry, bakehouse and smithy.

Geoffreye Museum, London Rooms of various times re-created.

Ham House, near Richmond Fine example of surviving furnishings, building and decorations.

Holyrood Palace, Edinburgh Home of Mary Queen of Scots for some time and also James I interest.

Museum of London, London Wall Models and exhibits, many things from the time.

National Maritime Museum, Greenwich Paintings of ships and also globes and navigational instruments of the period. Good pictures of ports and sea battles of the time.

National Portrait Gallery, London Many paintings from the time, including the monarchs.

Penshurst Place, Kent Civil War armour collection.

Royal Hospital, Chelsea Designed by Sir Christopher Wren.

Royal Hospital, Kilmainham, Dublin, Eire A retirement home for soldiers, built in 1687, with grand courtyards and squares.

Saint Paul's Cathedral, London Designed by Sir Christopher Wren.

Tower of London Many people were imprisoned there. Good collection of armour and weapons.

Victorian and Albert Museum, London Good examples of costumes and tapestries.

Westminster Abbey Crownings and burials of monarchs.

Woolsthorpe, Lincolnshire Isaac Newton's birthplace.

Index